Old Crianlarich, Tyndrum and Bri

by Bernard Byrom

A six-coach stopping train bound from Oban to Glasgow runs through Glen Dochart between Crianlarich and Killin Junction. The locomotive is one of the '191' class 4-6-0 tender engines designed for the Caledonian Railway by its Chief Mechanical Engineer, William Pickersgill, and built for them by the North British Locomotive Company at its Springburn Works in December 1922. In January 1923 the various railways were grouped into the 'Big Four' and the Caledonian became part of the London, Midland & Scottish Railway (LMS). These engines were not particularly successful and had a relatively short working life, the LMS scrapping the eight members of the class between 1939 and 1945. The River Dochart is flowing alongside the train and the bridge in the background leads to Lochdochart House on the north side of the river. The road on the left is the present-day A85.

First published in the United Kingdom, 2006,
by Stenlake Publishing Ltd.
Telephone: 01290 551122
www.stenlake.co.uk
ISBN 9781840333725

Lochdochart House has a long history. The Campbells of Breadalbane originally owned Glen Dochart but in 1825 the estate was sold to the Place family from Yorkshire who subsequently added the lands of Auchessan. In 1906 they sold the Glen Dochart part of the estate to the Christie family who are now celebrating a century of ownership of this characterful house. The photograph is dated 1914 when William Christie owned the house and had modified the original porch. The girl is thought to be Lillian Bell, a cousin of the owner, who was on holiday there. The trees surrounding the house became too big and were cut down in 1932 but many have since regrown.

Further Reading

The books listed below were used by the author during his research. None are available from Stenlake Publishing; please contact your local bookshop or reference library.

John Carmichael, *The Pilgrims Guide to Glencoe and Loch Awe*, 1859.
William A. Gillies, *In Famed Breadalbane*, 1938.
Seton Gordon, *Highways and Byways in the Central Highlands*, 1935.
Hugh Macmillan, *The Highland Tay*, 1901.
John McGregor, *100 Years of the West Highland Railway*, 1994.
Archie McKerracher, *Perthshire in History and Legend*, 1988, revised 2000.
O.S. Nock, *The Caledonian Railway*, 1963.
Mrs Place, *A Guide to Crianlarich*, 1910.
John Thomas, *The Callander & Oban Railway*, 1966.
John Thomas, *The West Highland Railway*, 1965, updated by A.J.S. Paterson, 1984.
Tom Weir, *The Oban Line*, 1973.
Strathfillan and Glen Dochart in Bygone Days, printed by the 'Callander Adventurer'.
The Proceedings of the Society of Antiquaries of Scotland.
The Statistical Accounts of Scotland, 1791-1799, 1845 and 1952.
Leslie's Directories, 1897-1940.
Valuation Rolls of the County of Perth, 1855 onwards.
The National Archives of Scotland, Edinburgh.

INTRODUCTION

The scope of this book covers only about 25 linear miles of country but comprises three very different geographical areas. The first part, from the Lix Toll near the foot of the northbound descent from Glenoglehead, goes westwards through Glen Dochart to the village of Crianlarich. Although there was an inn here in mid-Victorian times at the junction of the roads from Stirling via Glen Dochart and from Glasgow via Loch Lomond and Glen Falloch, the village did not even merit a mention in either the first or second editions of the *Statistical Account of Scotland*. It was not until the coming of the Callander & Oban Railway in 1873, followed twenty-one years later by the West Highland Railway, that Crianlarich achieved its present size and popularity with visitors.

In contrast to the lochs and wooded countryside of Glen Dochart, for the next five miles heading northwest to Tyndrum the countryside broadens out into the wide valley of Strathfillan where the River Fillan meanders gently across a marshy plain. This is an area associated with early Scottish history, from the Holy Pool where the eighth century Saint Fillan is said to have preached and effected miraculous cures on invalids, to the Field of Dalrigh where King Robert the Bruce fought a desperate battle against the MacDougalls of Lorne and their allies in 1306.

The village of Tyndrum is situated at the further end of Strathfillan. It has become more developed in recent years and is nowadays a popular service point for motor tourists and for walkers on the West Highland Way which passes through the centre of the village before heading northwards on the old military road towards Bridge of Orchy and Rannoch Moor. In the village it crosses the Coast-to-Coast Walk from Oban to St Andrews. The village owes its early existence to two major factors: one was its situation at the junction of the drove roads from the north and west to central Scotland and the other was its geological features which, over the centuries, have yielded metals ranging from lead to gold and silver.

The third section of the book heads northwards from Tyndrum through Bridge of Orchy and ends on the shores of Loch Tulla. As far as Bridge of Orchy the modern road generally runs parallel to both General Wade's old military road and the West Highland Railway, but at one point the railway takes a detour round the slopes of Beinn Dorain on the famous Horseshoe Curve.

In past times various clans, notably the MacGregors, owned much of the area covered by the book. However, during the sixteenth and seventeenth centuries most of these lands came into the possession of the Campbells of Breadalbane who acquired them by fair means or foul, usually the latter in the time of Sir Colin Campbell, who became the sixth Laird in 1550, and his son, the ruthless Sir Duncan Campbell, who was known as Black Duncan of the Cowl. At the beginning of the twentieth century the Marquis of Breadalbane was the greatest landowner in Britain and owned lands that stretched unbroken from Kenmore at the east end of Loch Tay through to Oban. However, various factors such as two world wars and penal rates of death duties caused the Breadalbane estate to be broken up and nowadays all the lands are owned by various private individuals and by the Forestry Commission.

The area as far as the county march boundary with Argyll north of Tyndrum is situated in Killin Parish. The first *Statistical Account*, written by the Rev. Patrick Stewart in the 1790s, tells us that the ground ranged from fertile plains in Glen Dochart and Strathfillan to the bare upper slopes of Ben More and Beinn Dorain. The area of Strathfillan and even the higher parts of the parish were once well wooded and in olden times the area around Ben More was a deer forest; it was later converted into a sheep-walk. People were generally very healthy and many lived to the age of 70 or 80 and even longer, but rheumatism was very prevalent because of the generally damp climate.

The principal crops produced in the parish were oats, peas, potatoes, flax and bear (coarse barley) but these were insufficient to supply the needs of the parish so quantities of meal had to be imported from the south. Labour rates had greatly increased in recent years and male labourers were by then paid 1/- per day when they provided their own victuals. A carpenter was paid 1/6d to 2/- per day; a tailor 1/- without meat or 8d with it; domestic menservants received from £7 to £10 per year and women from £2 to £4 per year.

At this time Clifton was the only town in the parish apart from Killin and the *Statistical Account* reported that it contained about 200 persons who principally worked in the mines. Lead had been mined at Clifton for the past 40 years but had temporally been given up, to the detriment of the poorer inhabitants of the village whose livelihoods depended upon it. The only inn was at Tyndrum, which was a posting stage between Killin and Dalmally. Apart from the miners at Clifton the inhabitants of the parish were principally weavers, tailors, shoemakers, wrights and flax dressers. The area had not escaped the Highland Clearances; it had been depopulated within the past 60 years and the crofters had been replaced by about 27,000 sheep, principally in the higher parts of the parish. Gaelic was still the language generally spoken in the area, but most of the younger people could understand something of the English language and could converse in it. They made a practice of going to serve in the Lowlands for several years, principally for the purpose of learning English.

The Rev. Joseph MacIntyre compiled the first *Statistical Account* of the parish of Glenorchy and Inishail, which covers the Bridge of Orchy area, in the 1790s. Whilst his account is in a similar vein to his counterpart at Killin, he took a dim view both of women smoking and of his parishioners drinking whisky. He wrote: 'Exclusive of what is sold by hawkers, there is sold yearly from one stationary shop in the village, to the sum of £60 Sterling, of snuff and tobacco. Let the men, however, continue to do this as they choose, but far be it from the fair and respectable females of this vale, to disfigure their features, and to destroy their powers of song and sweet cadence, by a habit so repugnant to everything engaging and cleanly in woman. There is one licensed distillery in the parish; the effect of which is the destruction of great quantities of grain that, instead of being converted into wholesome bread, produces only a deleterious spirit, ruinous to health, to industry and to morals.'

He mentioned that wages in the district had quadrupled over the last 50 years and went on to say: 'Often, especially during winter, whilst the men pass away the long evenings at their ease and without furthering the interest of their employers, the busy and conscientious housemaid is unremittingly engaged in some necessary employment in the family. Let not their earnings then, advanced as they are, be grudged; but let all who respect the female character and female utility regret that these earnings are often thrown away on the geegaws of vanity and fashion. Every man of humanity is pleased to see them clad in decent and suitable apparel; but it is painful to observe that, what should be a support to their future families and a provision for sickness and old age, is misapplied in the purchase of silks, laces, lawns and tinsel!' Given the present-day state pensions crisis, Chancellor Gordon Brown himself could hardly have phrased it better! The minister then goes on to say: 'But the moralist may speculate on this female infirmity as he chooses; as far as the lass has cash or credit to procure braws she will, step by step, follow hard after what she deems grand and fine in her betters'. Whew!

Very little appears to have changed by the time the *New Statistical Account* was written around fifty years later (in 1843), except that the price of labour had increased considerably.

Domestic menservants now received from £12 to £15 per year and women from £5 to £7 per year whilst a labourer could now earn 1/2d to 1/6d per day without victuals and a tradesman from 2/6d to 3/-. The standard of husbandry was rapidly improving, as were the houses, and the roads and bridges were said to be in excellent repair. The English language was slowly gaining ground although the majority of people still conversed in Gaelic. Peat was the most common fuel because it cost 3/- a cartload compared with £1 10/- for a ton of coal. The Marquis of Breadalbane, together with his relations, was still the biggest landowner by far but a few outsiders such as the Place family from Yorkshire had begun to purchase estates in the area.

The latter part of the nineteenth century saw the arrival in Strathfillan of two railways, the Callander & Oban and the West Highland. Their lines ran on opposite sides of the strath and they built their separate stations at both Crianlarich and Tyndrum. The Callander & Oban's line south of Crianlarich, together with its station there, was closed in 1965 but Tyndrum still has the distinction of being a small village with two stations on separate routes. The area has always been sparsely populated and the *Third Statistical Account* in 1952 described Crianlarich and Tyndrum as having 111 houses between them with a population of 225 adults and 75 children. As regards road transport, the A82 road through the district has been upgraded over the years and some of the locations in the book have been bypassed or modernised almost beyond recognition, but sharp-eyed travellers can still pick out most of them.

Acknowledgements

The author wishes to thank the following for their assistance during the research of this book: Mary Anderson, Tyndrum; Mackie Brodie, Tyndrum; John Burton, Dalrigh House, Tyndrum; Angus Cameron, Lochearnhead; Anne Cameron, Comrie; John and Seona Christie, Lochdochart House, Crianlarich; Irene Henderson, Crianlarich; Local History Library staff, A.K. Bell Library, Perth; Jim MacIntosh, Caledonian Railway Association; Colin McRae, Invervey Hotel, Tyndrum; Steve, Jan and Christine at Perthshire Archives, A.K. Bell Library, Perth; and Fulton and Mabel Ronald, The Old Church, Dalrigh, Tyndrum.

This is a view of the rear of Portnellan House, looking across Glen Dochart to Craig Liaragan and with Ben More farm on the right. Benmore Burn flows past the trees on the left, past the front of the house and into Loch Dochart at the foot of the hill. The house was originally built in the mid-nineteenth century as a shooting lodge for the Marquis of Breadalbane and later became a farm owned by William Christie of Lochdochart. It was devastated by a major fire in the early 1930s and this picture shows the house after it had been rebuilt. Since the 1980s a number of high quality holiday chalets have been built beyond the trees to the left of the house.

The castle on the island on Loch Dochart was built over the years between 1583 and 1631 by Sir Duncan Campbell (c.1553-1631), known as 'Black Duncan of the Cowl', and cost him 2,000 marks. It was built not as a defensive castle but as a three-storey tower house because it was felt to be secure on its island. However, the castle was captured in 1646 during the Civil War by the Marquis of Montrose, but was burnt when the Campbells subsequently recaptured it. In the early nineteenth century the estate was bought from them by Edward Place of Skelton Grange, York, after his marriage to Lady Ann Gordon. The castle remained completely buried in its own ruins until around 1890 when the Place family began to clear the undergrowth; amongst the discoveries they made was a dungeon eight feet deep which contained a quantity of charred bones. The castle and island are now owned by the Christie family of Lochdochart who have taken steps over the years to preserve the ruins for posterity.

Built as a private house for himself by Joseph Stewart, who ran the hotels at Crianlarich and Tyndrum, this house at Alltchaorain on the Glen Dochart road near Crianlarich is nowadays a well-known bed and breakfast establishment that has won top awards. The house in the foreground is no longer in existence. The mountain in the background is Ben Challum, the Gaelic name of which translates as 'Callum's Hill'. Rising to a height of 3,354 feet, it is a relatively easy Munro to climb when approached from the direction of the Kirkton Farm and past the ruins of St Fillan's Priory in Strathfillan.

This is the Inverardran farmhouse which stands on the left hand side of the A85 road approaching Crianlarich from Glen Dochart. It has had a variety of owners over the years and is nowadays a bed and breakfast establishment. A low-rise extension has been added to the right-hand side of the building and much of the vegetation has gone, but otherwise it appears unchanged from the time of this photograph.

The playing field in the foreground of this long-distance view of Crianlarich from across the River Fillan was abandoned long ago to its original environment of bog and rushes. The building in the centre with the long white roof is the Caledonian Railway's station on its line from Glasgow Buchanan Street to Oban via Stirling and Callander. On the right is the Church of Scotland building which at that time served only Crianlarich but which is nowadays the Strathfillan Parish Church. The Gaelic name of the village, A'Chrion Laraich, means 'low pass'. The village is situated where two military roads met; one came from Stirling via Callander and Glen Dochart and approached the village from the east on what is today the A85, the other came north from Dumbarton and approached via Glen Falloch on the modern-day A82. When two competing railways arrived from the south in late Victorian times, they too followed these same routes and converged at Crianlarich.

Prominent on the right of this view of Crianlarich, looking towards a misty Ben More, is the Church of Scotland building; its external appearance is unchanged today. On its left is the gabled building of the police station which was demolished and replaced by a new building on the same site in February 1969; next to that are the Caledonian Railway's station yard and buildings. The shop on the corner of the station yard belonged to the Caledonian Railway which leased it to George Hamilton who ran it for many years. Nowadays, nothing remains of the Caledonian's railway station and its associated buildings. A modern Londis store, incorporating the village post office, has been built in the left foreground of the picture, at the foot of the road which leads up to the high level station.

The A85 main road runs into the picture from Glen Dochart past the houses on the left. The nearest of these houses is 'Craigbank', which used to be owned by the Hamilton family who ran the store at the Caledonian station, but is nowadays a guest house. The house beyond it is 'Glenardran House' which is also a bed and breakfast establishment. The building on the right, which was the village post office at the time of this 1920s photograph, is now the centre part of the 'Rod and Reel' pub.

This Victorian view of the east end of the village looking towards Killin shows, on the right, the row of terraced cottages that was built by the North British Railway in 1894 for staff employed at its high level station which is just out of sight on the right of the picture. The gabled building beyond the houses is the old police station and, behind it, is the old school. Both were demolished and replaced in 1969. The entrance to the rival Caledonian Railway's low-level station is on the left of the road, just beyond the pony and trap. The white building in the distance on the opposite side of the road is the post office, now part of the 'Rod and Reel' pub. The quiet road itself is nowadays the busy A85 road through the village.

A view of the railway cottages taken from the opposite direction with what is now the A85 road entering the village from the east. The cottages are now on the left of the picture with the road leading to the North British Railway's high-level station immediately before them. The viaduct carries this railway line onwards to Tyndrum, Rannoch Moor, Fort William and Mallaig. The driveway leading off to the right led to the Caledonian Railway's low-level station. Beyond it, on the same side of the main road, is a short terrace of what may once have been cottages and then stables: they were subsequently converted into garages for the Crianlarich Hotel which is visible further down the road through the arch of the viaduct. The newer building on the right, known as 'The Evergreen', is the then recently built United Free Church Mission Station of Crianlarich. It was opened in 1910 but closed in 1929 when the Free Church united with the Church of Scotland; it now provides staff quarters for the hotel.

This is a later photograph of the scene in the last-but-one picture, taken from the railway viaduct looking eastwards towards Glen Dochart. By this time the railway cottages had their gardens extended out into the roadway but otherwise look the same. On the opposite side of the road the elongated building is the village hall which was replaced by the present hall in 1989, whilst in the foreground the old buildings in the previous picture have now been converted into lock-up garages for the benefit of guests staying at the Crianlarich Hotel. Other buildings in the picture are the village school (made up of the white building above centre and the building with the small cupola) and, just in front of it, the gable end of the police station. All were subsequently demolished, then rebuilt and reopened on 26 February 1969. At the far end of the picture the post office, now part of the 'Rod and Reel' pub, can be seen just before the bend in the road.

The Crianlarich Hotel was built in the centre of the village where the road from Glasgow via Glen Falloch (now the A82) joins the road from Perth and Stirling via Glen Dochart (now the A85). This picture shows the view looking west from the railway viaduct. In late Victorian times both this hotel and the Royal Hotel at Tyndrum were leased by Joseph Stewart, who also ran the famous Refreshment Rooms at the North British Railway's high-level station. The hotel is nowadays owned by Highland Heritage Ltd and specialises in being a base for their coach tour holidays. The left-hand section of the hotel in the picture is now covered with a brown metal cladding but the building as a whole is still recognisable. The building in the bottom right-hand corner of the picture, with petrol pumps standing beside it, is the former Toll House which is situated at the junction of the two main roads.

Several generations of the Stewart family ran the Crianlarich Hotel before it was finally sold to Ian Cleaver of the Highland Heritage hotel group which owns four hotels in the area. Its advertised facilities in the early years of the twentieth century included brown trout fishing in Lochs Dochart and Iubhair and in the River Fillan. It also had a nine-hole golf course that had been laid out by the famous golfer Willie Fernie, winner of the Open in 1883 and runner-up four times; in 1878 he had designed the championship course at Troon. To complement its up-to-date facilities, by the 1920s the hotel also had a garage and petrol pumps, and was the local headquarters of the Automobile Club (which, with the prefix 'Royal', later became the R.A.C.). This picture appears to date from the 1930s. The nearest cottage on the left is the former Toll House which has since been demolished. The cottage beyond it, which still stands, is 'Glen Bruar'.

This photograph was taken around the same period and from the same position as the previous one. Most of the people in the picture appear to be affluent visitors; note the uniformed chauffeur in the foreground, the well-dressed gentleman in plus-fours standing near him and the lady in an elegant fur coat standing by the motor car on the left. A tour coach with a fold-back roof waits in the background to collect its passengers after their lunch at the hotel. The railway viaduct in the background carries the line to Fort William; the railway still plays an important role in the local economy, but by the time the photograph was taken the motorcar and road coach were already making significant inroads into the railway's previous monopoly on holiday traffic.

A view of Crianlarich in winter, taken from outside the hotel with the former Toll House in the foreground. Next to it is 'Glen Bruar' and beyond the viaduct is the former United Free Church that is nowadays the hotel staff quarters. In the background is snow-capped Ben More.

This wood-built Scottish Youth Hostel was situated just below the high-level station which can be seen in the background. After many years service it was closed in the 1990s and a new hostel was built in stone a short distance to the north of the old building, the site of which is now occupied by a children's playground.

Youth hostelling has always provided a great opportunity for young people from different backgrounds and countries to learn about their fellow hostellers' cultures and music. In this picture a newcomer (in Sassenach clothing) appears to be enjoying his induction into Scottish country dancing, aided and abetted by a piper and an encouraging circle of fellow hostellers.

The approach to the Caledonian Railway's low-level station around the turn of the twentieth century. The main road eastwards towards Glen Dochart runs from left to right through the picture; the wooden buildings at the roadside were stables for the railway horses. The grocers shop and general store in the picture was run by the Hamilton family whose home was 'Craigbank', which is the furthest house visible down the road towards Killin. After the station's closure in 1965 the goods yard was retained as a timber loading depot but this too closed around 2005 and its business was transferred to the high-level station. The ground has been cleared and nothing now remains of this once busy yard but there are now plans afoot to build a new timber–loading depot here. The photograph was taken from Strathmore Terrace with the end of the row of railway cottages visible on the left. The gable of the old police station is on the right, with the road up to the high-level station passing on the far side of the white fence. The empty space on the far side of the fence is now occupied by a modern Londis store and post office.

A 1914 photograph of the Caledonian Railway's station, looking east towards Glen Dochart and Callander. The Callander & Oban Railway eventually reached Crianlarich in 1873, having spent the previous three years at a temporary terminus at Glenoglehead because it had run out of money. This Glenoglehead terminus had been named Killin although it was about five miles from that village; horse-drawn coaches had met the trains there to take passengers to hotels in that village. After the line was extended to Crianlarich and then onwards to Tyndrum in 1873 the Glenoglehead station was closed to passengers and subsequently, when a branch line to Killin - financed by the people of Killin themselves - was opened in 1886, an interchange station with the main line, named Killin Junction, was built out in the wilds of Glen Dochart. The Caledonian Railway's station at Crianlarich was built at street level and had reasonably good facilities for passengers on its northbound platform. Both this station and the North British Railway's station on the hillside were a great focus for outdoor men on the Sunday excursions of the 1930s when the return fare from Glasgow was 4/- (20p). This station, together with the whole section of line from Dunblane, was intended to be closed to passenger traffic in November 1965, but its actual closure was brought forward to 25 September by a massive landslip which blocked the line in Glen Ogle.

The West Highland Railway officially opened throughout from Craigendoran to Fort William on 11 August 1894. After traversing Glen Falloch the line reached Crianlarich where the West Highland built its own station, pictured here in the early years of the twentieth century looking west. Just beyond the water tanks on the left of the picture the railway crossed the Caledonian Railway's Oban line on a high level viaduct There was a connecting spur between the two lines but this was never used by regular passenger trains until the Glen Ogle landslide permanently closed the Caledonians line east of Crianlarich in 1965 and the Oban services were thereafter routed over the Glen Falloch line. The white letters showing the station's name on the side of the cutting have gone (or are buried in the undergrowth) and so have the water towers at the far end of the station that used to supply water for the locomotives, but otherwise the station has not changed much. The goods yard is still there and is used extensively by lorries bringing logs from local plantations for loading onto specially constructed rail wagons.

The house of Stronua stands in splendid isolation just outside Crianlarich on the A82 road heading towards Glen Falloch. The old military road through the glen can be seen running across the picture at the foot of the hill; it now forms part of the West Highland Way. Originally built as a farmhouse, this 1930s picture shows Stronua at a time when it was owned by the Malloch family and offered bed and breakfast accommodation. The curious building on the left was a former single-decker bus, minus its wheels, that had been converted into a roadside shop and tearoom named 'The Cyclists Rest' - after pedalling up Glen Falloch cyclists certainly needed a rest! The appearance of the house is almost unchanged today. The corrugated lean-to addition on the right hand gable has gone and has been replaced by a smaller and neater extension on the left-hand side, whilst no trace whatsoever remains of the old bus.

Strathfillan is the five-mile-long valley between the villages of Crianlarich and Tyndrum. Carved out by an Ice Age glacier, its lower end at Crianlarich divides into Glen Dochart which runs east towards Loch Tay and Glen Falloch which runs south towards Loch Lomond. Similarly, the Tyndrum end divides into Glen Orchy which carries the road to Fort William and Glen Lochy, the route to Oban. Unlike these narrower glens, Strathfillan is almost level and relatively wide and boggy. It was in this area in the eighth century that St Fillan, an Irish Christian missionary, made his home and is said to have performed miraculous feats of healing. Robert the Bruce built a priory at the place where the saint lived and its ruins can still be seen today by the side of the West Highland Way near Kirkton Farm. In this photograph the River Fillan is meandering down the Strath towards the outskirts of Crianlarich. The houses are still there but nowadays have many more neighbours, the area having become quite built-up.

Harvest time long ago at Auchreoch Farm, which stands on the left of the main road heading north-west towards Tyndrum. The Callander & Oban Railway line runs straight across the middle of the photograph. The Buchanan family came to Auchreoch in 1916 and are gathered in front of the farmhouse for the photograph. They sold the farm in 1955 and nowadays it is owned by Major Cruickshank; the farmhouse itself is unchanged from its appearance here.

Whilst the Callander & Oban Railway's line westwards was able to keep to the southern side of Strathfillan en-route to Tyndrum and only had to make one diversion to avoid a hostile landowner's salmon pool, the West Highland Railway's line to Fort William needed to climb the hillside towards Tyndrum before reaching its summit at the march boundary where it crossed from Perthshire into Argyll. At Auchtertyre in Strathfillan, the engineers were forced to take the line in a wide sweep to the north in order to cross the burn flowing down from Gleann a Chlachain on the long girder viaduct pictured here. The River Fillan flows through the foreground from left to right; the burn joined it just out of sight to the left of the picture. The Burton family, who still live nearby, were tenants of Auchtertyre farm from 1902 until 1935 when they moved across the road to Cononish. Auchtertyre is nowadays owned by SEERAD (Scottish Executive for Environment and Rural Affairs Department) and is farmed from the branch of the Scottish Agricultural College based in the white house.

When St Fillan came to the Strathfillan area early in the eighth century he built a church at Auchentyre and blessed the nearby pool on the river; consequently it became known as the 'Holy Pool'. It was claimed to have healing powers and was particularly famous for curing the mentally ill who visited it in large numbers over the centuries. An allegedly insane person would be immersed in the pool, then taken half a mile to the churchyard where they were secured to a stone and had St Fillan's bell placed over their heads. If they broke loose by the next morning it was a sign that they had been cured. If they were unsuccessful they were considered incurable. When St Fillan died he was buried in Strathfillan but subsequently one of his relics was taken to Bannockburn where it was claimed to have helped Robert the Bruce in his victory over the English. In gratitude, Bruce later founded a priory in Strathfillan in the saint's honour; its ruins are still visible today. At one time St Fillan's staff and bell were kept at the church, but the bell was illegally taken to England by a tourist in 1798 and was not returned to Scotland until 1869 (whether the bell actually dates from St Fillan's time is unclear; the first record of its existence dates from the 1400s although it is thought to be much older). In later years the church and manse pictured here were built at the side of the main road. Nowadays, this section of the road has been bypassed by the modern A82 and is now a private road. In time the church and manse themselves became redundant and have now been converted into a private dwelling. The buildings on the right of the picture are Dalrigh House and the former Free Church, both of which are described in the next two pages.

This photograph dates from around 1900 and shows the Field of Dalrigh, (pronounced *Dalree*), which means the 'King's Field'. This field is the site of an encounter in 1306 when, having been defeated at the Battle of Methven, Robert the Bruce and his followers took refuge in this area and their whereabouts became known to the MacDougalls of Lorne who had a blood feud against him. In the ensuing skirmish Bruce was lucky to escape with his life. During the fight one of the men of Lorne caught hold of Bruce's plaid; his grip was so tight that Bruce could only escape by releasing his plaid and, in doing so, lost the fastening brooch of the plaid. The brooch remains a trophy of the MacDougalls to this day. As Bruce and his followers retreated eastwards they are said to have thrown their weapons into a nearby lochan which thereby gained the name Lochan-an-arm, the 'Loch of the Weapons'. The building on the right was a church established in 1829 by the Society in Scotland for Propagating Christian Knowledge (SSPCK). Following the 'Disruption' in 1843, which led to the formation of the Free Church of Scotland, it became the local Free Church but was made redundant in 1929 when the United Free Church made up its differences with the Established (Presbyterian) Church, the two of them uniting into today's Church of Scotland. The church and manse at Strathfillan (see previous picture) were completely renovated and services were continued there. The former Free Church was closed, used as a barn for many years and then converted into a private house in 2002 by Mr and Mrs Ronald. The building beyond it is the former manse but, after five of the Rev. Fraser's children died there from tuberculosis, a new manse was built in Tyndrum which nowadays forms the principal part of the Invervey Hotel.

The building in the foreground in this 1929 photograph is Strathfillan school which served the whole of the local area. It was probably built shortly before the First World War and the former manse was refurbished to serve as a house for its first schoolmaster, Mr Grewer. The road running in front of it was, at that time, the main A82 road and in 1965 parents demanded that a safety barrier should be erected to guard against traffic crashing into the playground. This was done, but when the parents also demanded that either the playground should be asphalted and the toilet facilities improved or that the school should be closed and children taken by bus to the school in Crianlarich, the education authorities decided that the latter option was preferable. The school, which had one teacher and only twelve scholars, was closed and demolished and only a rusty fence now shows where it once stood. The site of the school is nowadays bypassed by a new section of the A82. The building in the picture nearest to the school is the former SSPCK church of 1829. Beyond it is its former manse, owned by the Burton family since 1968 and nowadays named 'Dalrigh House'; on its left is the bungalow named 'Ardormie' which was built in 1923 by Mr Grewer on his retirement from teaching.

At last the tearoom pictured on the cover appears to have a customer! The road running past the shop is the former A82 road heading north-west towards Tyndrum. This section of the road has nowadays been bypassed by a modern road which runs into the area pictured from the centre right, heading to Tyndrum which lies in the hollow between the hills. The old road crosses the River Cononish on the stone bridge (known locally as the 'White Bridge') in the centre of the picture and winds its way past the Field of Dalrigh to join the line of the modern road. The bridge can no longer be used by motor vehicles, but walkers still have access and the West Highland Way passes nearby. The Cononish rises on the slopes of nearby Ben Lui; shortly beyond this bridge it becomes the River Fillan and beyond Crianlarich it becomes the River Dochart up to where it flows into the head of Loch Tay. Thus, it can truly be said to be the principal source of the mighty River Tay. The route of the West Highland Railway can be discerned by the line of trees on the upper right of the picture as it climbs the hillside towards Upper Tyndrum Station. The buildings above the bridge on the far side of the Field of Dalrigh have already been described in detail on previous pages.

The name Tyndrum is derived from the Gaelic *Tigh an Druim* which means 'the house on the ridge'. The name is quite appropriate as the village lies on a geographical watershed which means that the waters on one side of the village run off to the west whereas those on the other side run off to the east. Beinn Dorain (3,524 feet), in the centre of the picture, overshadows Tyndrum in this photograph, taken at a time when the village consisted of only a few houses on the east side of the burn and a street of old houses at Clifton on the west. At the time the photograph was taken, the house amongst the trees in the centre was the Free Church manse, although it has since become the Invervey Hotel and the shop on its left has now been transformed into the Green Welly Stop. The main road through Strathfillan passes in front of both these buildings and then crosses the burn on a stone bridge. Here the road divided; the one to Oban carried straight on to the left of the picture whilst the old military road to Fort William which enters at the bottom of the picture can be seen climbing north towards Bridge of Orchy. The Caledonian Railway's station on the Oban line, opened in August 1873, is in the foreground. The village may have been small but it was located at the meeting point of two major cattle drove roads from the north and west and was therefore an important place for loading cattle onto trucks for destinations further south. The cattle-loading bank can be seen to the left of the station.

Photographed in 1920, Mr Angus Fraser and his family pose proudly outside their general store and post office at Tyndrum. At this time their shop was virtually the only one for miles around. The building was subsequently enlarged and in 1965 it became the Clifton Coffee House & Craft Centre. Situated near the junction of the roads to Oban and Fort William, as well as lying on both the West Highland Way and the east-west Coast-to-Coast Walk from Oban to St Andrews, it became popular with a wide range of tourists. Nowadays Mr Fraser's shop, much altered, forms a section of this greatly enlarged store, which changed its name in 2000 to The Green Welly Stop and nowadays includes a restaurant and petrol filling station.

The Royal Hotel at Tyndrum was built in Victorian times as a coaching inn where horses could be changed whilst passengers dined before continuing their journeys to Oban or Fort William. One of its distinguished visitors was the poet Samuel Taylor Coleridge, who dined here on his way to Fort William in 1803. For many years from Victorian times the hotel was leased by the Stewart family who also owned the Crianlarich Hotel. When the motoring era arrived they offered garaging and petrol pump facilities to this new breed of travellers and their premises was the local headquarters of the Automobile Club. In 1931 a fire destroyed the part of the hotel on the left-hand side of the picture.

In this 1930s photograph the Royal Hotel's buildings have been extended to accommodate motor coach tour parties. Like its sister hotel in Crianlarich, the Royal is nowadays owned by Highland Heritage Ltd who use it as a base for their coach parties which come from the length and breadth of Britain to enjoy the delights of the Highlands. In spite of a modern covered entrance approach and a low-rise lounge built onto the front of the hotel, the building is still easily recognisable from both the earlier and later photographs.

The Callander & Oban line reached Tyndrum in 1873, and halted here for four years until enough money was raised to continue its construction westwards to Dalmally and Oban. Rail passengers had to alight here and continue their journeys by horse-drawn coaches. The railway eventually reached Oban in 1880. The entire station staff are posing for this photograph, whilst two lady passengers sit patiently on the platform bench. The poster on the end of the building is advertising sailings on Loch Tay to Kenmore which would have been reached via Killin Junction and the branch line from there to Loch Tay Pier. The station is still open but the station buildings in the picture have been demolished and replaced by a very utilitarian modern platform with minimal facilities. The right-hand track has been taken up and the platform it served is no longer there, whilst the Killin branch and the sailings to Kenmore are now but a very distant memory.

This is a photograph of the Callander & Oban station at Tyndrum taken at a later date than the previous one, probably in the 1920s. It looks as though a train from Oban has just set down passengers at the right-hand platform and has left the station to continue its journey south-eastwards towards Crianlarich. The passengers are using the level crossing to leave the station and head for the village, quite unperturbed by the freight train's locomotive standing with steam up only a few feet away from the crossing. This was a routine procedure at the time and for many years afterwards, but is a scenario that would give today's Health & Safety Executive forty thousand fits! The platform on the right with its loop line and signal box is no longer there and only a single line now runs through the rebuilt station.

In contrast to the Callander & Oban line's station near the village centre, the West Highland line's station is situated on the hillside above the village and approached by a long, steep, road. Its situation was dictated by the necessity for the railway to climb along the hillside all the way from Crianlarich to the county march boundary between Perthshire and Argyll a few miles north of Tyndrum, from which summit it descended to Bridge of Orchy. In this 1952 photograph the train, which is heading from Fort William to Glasgow, appears to have set down two ladies who are waving farewell to the guard. The nearest carriage is a typical ex-LNER saloon but the last coach is one of the newer British Railways Mark 1 carriages which had then only recently been introduced into service. The scene at the station is unchanged today - even the original iron gates are still in position.

The former mining settlement of Clifton lies on the far side of the road bridge over the burn which joins with several others in the neighbourhood to form the River Fillan. In this picture the one-time village post office and stores, standing on the A82 main road by the bridge and now incorporated into the Green Welly Stop, is prominent on the right of the picture. On the left of the road bridge are the cottages that were built for miners working at the nearby lead mine and which follow the line of the old military road down as far as the bend in the river. Constructed in the 'butt and ben' style and with thatched roofs, most of these cottages are still standing apart from the nearest two. After crossing the bridge, the road branches into two - one branch going to the left and taking the western pass through the hills to Oban, whilst the old military road can be seen continuing northwards towards Glencoe and Fort William.

This 1913 view of the crossroads at Clifton shows the village from the opposite angle to the previous picture. The A82 main road enters from the left, having just crossed the bridge, and continues towards Dalmally and Oban. The photographer is standing at the foot of the old military road from Fort William which continues past the cottages on the far side of the road towards Dalrigh and onwards through Strathfillan. The row of old cottages on the far side of the crossroads have survived the years and look very similar today, but the thatched house in the foreground has been demolished and replaced by the modern building which nowadays houses the long-established Brodie's Stores. The two-storey house on the far side of the road was named 'Alma Cottage', although it no longer carries that name.

The nearest cottage in this tranquil Edwardian scene is 'Garden Cottage' which has a corrugated-iron roof. The cottage beyond it is 'Crombie'. It was the practice many years ago for householders to protect their thatched roofs with a covering of corrugated iron as a cheaper alternative to replacing the thatch with slate. 'Garden Cottage' still sports this covering today. The old military road runs in front of the cottages up to the bridge in the centre of the photograph where it crosses the Oban road and continues up the glen towards Bridge of Orchy on its way to Fort William.

Precious metals have been mined in this area since the fifteenth century. In 1428 enough silver was produced from the mine at Tyndrum for it to be declared a 'Royal Mine'. Around 1730 Sir Robert Clifton, who gave his name to the little mining settlement at Tyndrum, started mining commercially for lead and the mine has been worked in fits and starts ever since. For instance, in the late 1700s it gave employment to around 200 miners but was closed by the 1790s; in the 1840s the mine had re-opened under the supervision of experienced German miners and a large ore-crushing plant was erected near the main road, but by the 1890s it was again disused. Production restarted during the First World War but this did not continue for long after the war. Gold has also been mined in very small quantities on the far side of the hill. The mine is owned by Fynegold Exploration Ltd. but is currently dormant. Meanwhile, on the far side of the hill you can still find optimists panning for gold; occasionally they are lucky and find enough to make into small items of jewellery.

The River Orchy is well known for the quality of its salmon fishing and this fisherman of the 1930s is trying his luck on the river towards Bridge of Orchy. His everyday clothing suggests that he is fishing not so much for the sport as for his evening meal!

After leaving Tyndrum the West Highland line continues its steep climb up to the county march boundary, then runs on falling gradients to Bridge of Orchy with the old military road to Fort William running alongside for much of the way. The ground was not suitable for the railway line to be taken on an embankment directly across the valley from the hill in the foreground to the slopes of Beinn Dorain in the background. Instead the engineer, Charles Forman, was forced to make a detour round three sides of the mountains which resulted in what became known as the Horseshoe Curve. In this photograph the line can be seen on the right approaching the curve which is out of sight round the corner, and beyond, over on the left, running along the lower slopes of Beinn Dorain.

Auch Lodge stands on the plain near the Horseshoe Curve and in the shadow of Beinn Dorain. Whilst the main buildings appear unchanged today, some of its outbuildings have been converted into holiday cottages. The Gaelic name Beinn Dorain means 'hill of tempests', so called because there are several small glens which open up around its slopes and act like air vents, causing sudden violent squalls.

The village of Bridge of Orchy lies at the head of Glen Orchy and is six miles north of Tyndrum. This small settlement grew nearby the bridge over the River Orchy, which was built by General Caulfeild in 1751 as part of the military road to Fort William. The inn on the right became very popular with drovers and was also visited by Dorothy Wordsworth in 1803. It has since been extended but is still easily recognisable from this old photograph. The adjoining church also probably dates from the eighteenth century. In the 1870s Captain W.W. Mackie toured this area by pony cart in search of prime breeding stock for the Scotch Terrier dog. He was ultimately successful and the result of his breeding was 'Dundee' who is regarded as the prototype of the 'Scottie' dog we know today. Today the village is popular as a starting point for climbing two local Munros, Beinn Dorain at 3,524 feet and Beinn an Dothaidh at 3,267 feet, as well as canoeing and white-water rafting on the River Orchy.

This 1927 view of the bridge with the river in flood is looking upstream with the road leading to Inveroran on the left and the Bridge of Orchy Hotel just out of sight to the right. Between 1725 and 1767 General Wade and, later, Major Caulfeild built some 1,200 miles of military roads and 700 bridges throughout the Highlands. This old military road crosses the modern A82 at the crossroads in the centre of the village before descending past the hotel to this bridge over the River Orchy.

Bridge of Orchy Station is the first one beyond Tyndrum on the West Highland Railway line to Fort William and is situated only a few miles beyond the Horseshoe Curve. The station building is in typical Swiss Chalet style and is grade B listed. It is nowadays unmanned and its waiting room has been converted into a bunkhouse named the West Highland Way Sleeper and is run by Scottish Independent Hostels. When the line was being built the engineers proposed to supply the station with drinking water from a nearby mountain burn. The landowner, the Marquis of Breadalbane, objected unsuccessfully to the courts against the railway company entering his land and taking the water, but his objection was upheld in the House of Lords. This 1927 photograph shows that, as well as the station buildings themselves, there were also a number of other buildings connected with the railway such as the station master's house. The large goods wagon standing in the siding is a visitor from the (English) North Eastern Railway, although by that date it was part of the London & North Eastern Railway (LNER), whilst the ancient North British Railway carriage is presumably serving as a bothy for the local railwaymen. The road on the right is the old military road, nowadays part of the West Highland Way, on its way from Tyndrum to cross the River Orchy at the nearby bridge by the hotel.

Blackmount Lodge lies on the north side of Loch Tulla on a long private drive which branches off the old military road at Forest Lodge. It has long been owned by the Fleming family who are related to the late Ian Fleming, creator of James Bond.